Simple 1-2-3
Appetizers

Publications International, Ltd.

Pictured on the front cover: Southern Crab Cakes with Rémoulade Dipping Sauce *(page 23).*
Pictured on the back cover *(top to bottom):* Stout Beef Bundles *(page 7)* and Mediterranean Flatbread *(page 59).*

ISBN-13: 978-1-4127-9582-1
ISBN-10: 1-4127-9582-6

Library of Congress Control Number: 2008930604

Manufactured in China.

8 7 6 5 4 3 2 1

Microwave Cooking: Microwave ovens vary in wattage. Use the cooking times as guidelines and check for doneness before adding more time.

Preparation/Cooking Times: Preparation times are based on the approximate amount of time required to assemble the recipe before cooking, baking, chilling or serving. These times include preparation steps such as measuring, chopping and mixing. The fact that some preparations and cooking can be done simultaneously is taken into account. Preparation of optional ingredients and serving suggestions is not included.

Publications International, Ltd.

Contents

COMPANY'S COMING

Grilled Lobster, Shrimp and Calamari Seviche

Makes 6 servings

¾ cup orange juice
⅓ cup fresh lime juice
2 tablespoons tequila
2 jalapeño peppers,★
    seeded and minced
2 tablespoons chopped
    fresh cilantro or chives
1 teaspoon honey
1 teaspoon ground cumin
1 teaspoon olive oil
10 squid, cleaned and
    cut into rings and
    tentacles
½ pound medium raw
    shrimp, peeled and
    deveined
2 lobster tails (8 ounces
    each), meat removed
    and shells discarded

★Jalapeño peppers can sting and irritate the skin, so wear rubber gloves when handling peppers and do not touch your eyes.

1. Combine orange juice, lime juice, tequila, jalapeños, cilantro and honey in medium bowl. Measure ¼ cup marinade into small bowl; stir in cumin and oil. Reserve. Refrigerate remaining marinade.

2. Prepare grill for direct cooking. Bring 1 quart water to a boil in large saucepan over high heat. Add squid; cook 30 seconds or until opaque. Drain. Rinse under cold water; drain. Add squid to refrigerated marinade.

3. Thread shrimp onto metal skewers. Brush shrimp and lobster with reserved ¼ cup marinade. Place shrimp on grid. Grill shrimp, uncovered, over medium-hot coals 2 to 3 minutes per side or until pink and opaque. Remove shrimp from skewers; add to squid. Place lobster on grid. Grill 5 minutes per side or until meat turns opaque and is cooked through. Slice lobster meat into ¼-inch-thick slices; add to squid and shrimp mixture. Refrigerate at least 2 hours or overnight.

Stout Beef Bundles

Makes 8 servings

1 pound ground beef
½ cup sliced green onions
1 medium clove garlic,
　　minced
⅔ cup chopped water
　　chestnuts
½ cup chopped red bell
　　pepper
¼ cup stout
2 tablespoons hoisin sauce
1 tablespoon soy sauce
2 tablespoons chopped
　　fresh cilantro
1 or 2 heads leaf lettuce,
　　separated into leaves,
　　outer leaves discarded

1. Brown beef 6 to 8 minutes in large skillet over medium-high heat, stirring to break up meat. Drain fat. Add onions and garlic; cook and stir until tender.

2. Stir in water chestnuts, bell pepper, stout, hoisin and soy sauce. Cook, stirring occasionally, until bell pepper is crisp-tender and most liquid has evaporated. Remove from heat.

3. Stir in cilantro. Spoon ground beef mixture onto lettuce leaves; sprinkle with additional hoisin sauce, if desired. Wrap lettuce leaf around ground beef mixture to make appetizer bundle.

Tip: Slice additional green onions into long strips and use to tie lettuce leaves in place around bundles.

Vegetable & Couscous Filled Tomatoes

Makes 18 servings

½ cup chicken broth
2 teaspoons olive oil
⅓ cup uncooked quick-cooking couscous
18 large plum tomatoes
Nonstick cooking spray
1 cup diced zucchini
⅓ cup sliced green onions
2 cloves garlic, minced
2 tablespoons finely chopped fresh Italian parsley
1½ teaspoons Dijon mustard
½ teaspoon Italian seasoning

1. Place chicken broth and oil in small saucepan; bring to a boil over high heat. Stir in couscous; cover. Remove saucepan from heat; let stand 5 minutes. Cut thin slice from top of each tomato. Remove pulp, leaving ⅛-inch-thick shell; reserve pulp. Place tomatoes, cut sides down, on paper towels to drain. Meanwhile, drain excess liquid from reserved pulp. Chop pulp to measure ⅔ cup.

2. Spray large nonstick skillet with cooking spray; heat over medium heat. Add zucchini, onions and garlic. Cook and stir 5 minutes or until vegetables are tender.

3. Combine couscous, reserved tomato pulp, vegetables, parsley, mustard and Italian seasoning in large bowl. Fill tomato shells evenly with couscous mixture.

Brandy-Soaked Scallops

Makes 8 servings

1 pound bacon, cut in half crosswise
2 pounds small sea scallops
½ cup brandy
⅓ cup olive oil
2 tablespoons chopped fresh parsley
1 clove garlic, minced
1 teaspoon black pepper
½ teaspoon salt
½ teaspoon onion powder

1. Wrap one piece bacon around each scallop; secure with toothpick, if necessary. Place wrapped scallops in 13×9-inch baking dish.

2. Combine brandy, oil, parsley, garlic, pepper, salt and onion powder in small bowl; mix well. Pour mixture over scallops; cover and marinate in refrigerator at least 4 hours.

3. Remove scallops from marinade; discard marinade. Arrange scallops on rack of broiler pan. Broil 4 inches from heat 7 to 10 minutes or until bacon is browned. Turn; broil 5 minutes more or until scallops are opaque. Remove any toothpicks.

Roasted Eggplant Rolls

Makes 8 servings (16 rolls)

2 medium eggplants
(¾ pound each)
2 tablespoons lemon juice
1 teaspoon olive oil
4 tablespoons (2 ounces)
cream cheese
2 tablespoons sour cream
1 green onion, minced
4 sun-dried tomatoes
(packed in oil), rinsed,
drained and minced
1 clove garlic, minced
¼ teaspoon dried oregano
⅛ teaspoon black pepper
16 fresh stemmed spinach
leaves
1 cup meatless pasta sauce

1. Preheat oven to 450°F. Spray baking sheets with nonstick cooking spray; set aside. Trim ends from eggplants. Cut eggplants lengthwise into ¼-inch-thick slices (about 16 slices total). Discard outside slices that are mostly skin. Arrange slices in single layer on prepared baking sheets.

2. Combine lemon juice and olive oil in small bowl; brush lightly over both sides of eggplant slices. Bake 22 to 24 minutes or until slightly golden brown, turning once. Transfer eggplant slices to plate; cool. Meanwhile, stir together cream cheese, sour cream, green onion, sun-dried tomatoes, garlic, oregano and pepper in small bowl until blended.

3. Spread about 1 teaspoon cream cheese mixture evenly over each eggplant slice. Arrange spinach leaf on top, leaving ½-inch border. Roll up, beginning at small end. Lay rolls, seam side down, on serving platter. (If making ahead, cover and refrigerate up to 2 days. Bring to room temperature before serving.) Serve with warmed pasta sauce.

Savory Herb-Stuffed Onions

Makes 4 servings

1 zucchini, cut lengthwise into ¼-inch-thick slices
Nonstick cooking spray
3 shiitake mushrooms
4 large sweet onions
1 plum tomato, seeded and chopped
2 tablespoons fresh bread crumbs
1 tablespoon fresh basil *or* 1 teaspoon dried basil
1 teaspoon olive oil
¼ teaspoon salt
⅛ teaspoon black pepper
4 tablespoons water
4 teaspoons balsamic vinegar

1. Prepare grill for direct cooking. Spray zucchini slices with cooking spray. Grill, uncovered, over medium coals 4 minutes or until tender, turning once. Cut into 1-inch pieces; set aside. Thread mushrooms onto metal skewers. Grill, covered, over medium coals 20 to 30 minutes or until tender. Chop and set aside.

2. Remove stem and root ends of onions, leaving peels intact. Spray onions with cooking spray; grill, root end up, on covered grill over medium coals 5 minutes or until lightly charred. Remove and cool slightly. Peel and scoop about 1 inch of pulp from stem ends; chop pulp for filling.

3. Combine zucchini, mushrooms, chopped onion, tomato, bread crumbs, basil, oil, salt and pepper in large bowl; mix until blended. Spoon mixture evenly into onion centers. Place on sheets of foil; sprinkle each evenly with water. Wrap onions; seal foil. Grill onion packets on covered grill over medium coals 45 to 60 minutes or until tender. Spoon 1 teaspoon vinegar over each onion.

Spring Rolls

Makes 12 appetizers

1 cup pre-shredded cabbage or coleslaw mix
½ cup finely chopped cooked ham
¼ cup finely chopped water chestnuts
¼ cup thinly sliced green onions
3 tablespoons plum sauce, divided
1 teaspoon dark sesame oil
3 (6-inch) flour tortillas

1. Combine cabbage, ham, water chestnuts, onions, 2 tablespoons plum sauce and sesame oil in medium bowl. Mix well. Spread remaining 1 tablespoon plum sauce evenly over tortillas.

2. Spread about ¾ cup cabbage mixture on each tortilla to within ¼ inch of edge; roll up. Wrap each tortilla tightly in plastic wrap. Refrigerate at least 1 hour or up to 24 hours before serving.

3. To serve, cut each tortilla into 4 pieces.

Tip: Plum sauce is a sweet, jam-like sauce with a tart flavor. It is made with a combination of vinegar, sugar and other seasonings.

Spanish-Style Garlic Shrimp

Makes 6 servings

4 tablespoons I CAN'T
   BELIEVE IT'S NOT
   BUTTER!® Spread,
   divided
1 pound uncooked
   medium shrimp,
   peeled and deveined
½ teaspoon salt
2 cloves garlic, finely
   chopped
½ to 1 jalapeño pepper,★
   seeded and finely
   chopped
¼ cup chopped fresh
   cilantro or parsley
1 tablespoon fresh lime
   juice

★Jalapeño peppers can sting and
irritate the skin, so wear rubber
gloves when handling peppers and
do not touch your eyes.

In 12-inch nonstick skillet, melt
1 tablespoon I Can't Believe It's Not
Butter!® Spread over high heat and
cook shrimp with salt 2 minutes or
until shrimp are almost pink, turning
once. Remove shrimp and set aside.

In same skillet, melt remaining
3 tablespoons I Can't Believe It's
Not Butter!® Spread over medium-
low heat and cook garlic and
jalapeño pepper, stirring occasionally,
1 minute. Return shrimp to skillet.
Stir in cilantro and lime juice; heat
30 seconds or until shrimp turn pink.

Serve, if desired, with crusty Italian
bread.

Roasted Red Pepper and Artichoke Torte

Makes 20 servings

2½ cups chopped bagels (about 3 bagels)
2 tablespoons olive oil
2 packages (8 ounces each) cream cheese, softened
1 container (15 ounces) ricotta cheese
1 can (10¾ ounces) condensed cream of celery soup, undiluted
2 eggs
2 tablespoons chopped green onion
1 tablespoon Italian seasoning
1 clove garlic, minced
1 can (8½ ounces) artichoke hearts, drained and chopped
1 jar (15 ounces) roasted red bell peppers, drained, chopped and divided
1 cup chopped fresh basil, divided
Assorted crackers

1. Preheat oven to 375°F. Combine bagels and oil in medium bowl; mix well. Spray 9-inch springform baking pan with nonstick cooking spray. Press bagel mixture into bottom of prepared pan. Bake 15 minutes; cool.

2. Beat cheeses, soup, eggs, green onion, Italian seasoning and garlic with electric mixer at medium speed until well blended. Spread half of cheese mixture over bagel crust. Top with artichokes and half each of peppers and basil. Spread remaining cheese mixture over basil; top with remaining peppers.

3. Bake 1 hour or until center is set; cool. Refrigerate 6 to 8 hours or overnight. Run knife around edge of torte; remove side of pan. Top with remaining ½ cup basil. Thinly slice torte and serve with crackers.

Southern Crab Cakes with Rémoulade Dipping Sauce

Makes 8 servings

10 ounces fresh lump
    crabmeat
1½ cups fresh white or
    sourdough bread
    crumbs, divided
¼ cup chopped green
    onions
½ cup mayonnaise, divided
1 egg white, lightly beaten
2 tablespoons coarse
    grain or spicy brown
    mustard, divided
¾ teaspoon hot pepper
    sauce, divided
2 teaspoons olive oil,
    divided
    Lemon wedges
    (optional)

1. Preheat oven to 200°F. Pick out and discard any shell or cartilage from crabmeat. Combine crabmeat, ¾ cup bread crumbs and green onions in medium bowl. Add ¼ cup mayonnaise, egg white, 1 tablespoon mustard and ½ teaspoon hot pepper sauce; mix well. Using ¼ cup mixture per cake, shape into 8 (½-inch-thick) cakes. Roll crab cakes lightly in remaining ¾ cup bread crumbs.

2. Heat large nonstick skillet over medium heat; add 1 teaspoon oil. Add 4 crab cakes; cook 4 to 5 minutes per side or until golden brown. Transfer to serving platter; keep warm in oven. Repeat with remaining 1 teaspoon oil and crab cakes.

3. To prepare dipping sauce, mix remaining ¼ cup mayonnaise, 1 tablespoon mustard and ¼ teaspoon hot pepper sauce in small bowl until blended. Serve crab cakes warm with dipping sauce and lemon wedges.

Artichoke Frittata

Artichoke Frittata

Makes 12 to 16 servings

3 teaspoons extra-virgin
    olive oil, divided
½ cup minced green onions
5 eggs
1 can (14 ounces)
    artichoke hearts,
    drained and chopped
½ cup (2 ounces) shredded
    Swiss cheese
2 tablespoons grated
    Parmesan cheese
1 tablespoon minced fresh
    parsley
1 teaspoon salt
¼ teaspoon black pepper

1. Heat 2 teaspoons oil in large ovenproof skillet over medium heat. Add green onions; cook and stir until tender. Remove from skillet.

2. Whisk eggs in medium bowl until frothy. Stir in artichokes, green onions, cheeses, parsley, salt and pepper.

3. Heat remaining 1 teaspoon oil in same skillet over medium heat. Pour egg mixture into skillet. Cook 4 to 5 minutes or until bottom is lightly browned. Place large plate over skillet; invert frittata onto plate. Return frittata, uncooked side down, to skillet. Cook about 4 minutes or until center is just set. Cut into wedges to serve.

Smoked Salmon Appetizers

Makes 2 dozen appetizers

¼ cup cream cheese, softened
1 tablespoon chopped fresh dill *or* 1 teaspoon dried dill weed
⅛ teaspoon ground red pepper
4 ounces thinly sliced smoked salmon or lox
24 melba toast rounds or other crackers
Fresh dill sprigs and chopped red onion, (optional)

1. Combine cream cheese, dill and red pepper in small bowl; stir to blend. Spread evenly over each slice of salmon. Roll up salmon slices jelly-roll style. Place on plate; cover with plastic wrap. Chill at least 1 hour or up to 4 hours before serving.

2. Cut salmon rolls crosswise into ¾-inch pieces with sharp knife. Place rolls, cut side down, on melba toast.

3. Garnish each salmon roll with dill sprig and onion. Serve cold or at room temperature.

Tip: There are two distinct varieties of smoked salmon—hot smoked or kippered and cold smoked or Nova lox. The main differences between them are the brining process and also the temperature at which they are smoked. Hot smoked salmon is smoked at 145°F while cold smoked salmon is smoked at 80°F.

FILLED & SKEWERED

Leek Strudels

Makes 9 servings

Nonstick cooking spray
2 pounds leeks, cleaned and sliced (white parts only)
¼ teaspoon caraway seeds
¼ teaspoon salt
⅛ teaspoon white pepper
¼ cup chicken broth
3 sheets frozen phyllo dough, thawed
Butter-flavored nonstick cooking spray

1. Coat large skillet with nonstick cooking spray; heat over medium heat. Add leeks; cook and stir about 5 minutes or until tender. Stir in caraway seeds, salt and pepper. Add chicken broth; bring to a boil over high heat. Reduce heat to low. Simmer, covered, about 5 minutes or until broth is absorbed. Let mixture cool to room temperature.

2. Preheat oven to 400°F. Cut each sheet of phyllo dough lengthwise into thirds. Spray 1 piece phyllo dough with nonstick cooking spray; spoon 2 tablespoons leek mixture near bottom of piece. Fold 1 corner over filling to make triangle. Continue folding, as you would fold a flag, to make triangular packet.

3. Repeat with remaining phyllo dough and leek mixture. Place packets on ungreased baking sheet; lightly coat tops of packets with butter-flavored cooking spray. Bake about 20 minutes or until golden brown. Serve warm.

Tortellini Kabobs with Pesto Ranch Dip

Makes 6 to 8 servings

½ (16-ounce) bag frozen tortellini
1¼ cups prepared ranch salad dressing
½ cup grated Parmesan cheese
3 cloves garlic, minced
2 teaspoons dried basil

1. Cook tortellini according to package directions. Rinse and drain under cold water.

2. Thread tortellini onto wooden skewers (2 tortellini per skewer).

3. Combine salad dressing, cheese, garlic and basil in small bowl. Serve tortellini kabobs with dip.

SERVING SUGGESTION:
For another quick-to-prepare dip, combine prepared pasta sauce or salsa with finely chopped black olives.

Prep and Cook Time: 30 minutes

Chicken and Rice Puffs

Makes 6 servings

1 box frozen puff pastry shells, thawed

1 package (about 6 ounces) long grain and wild rice

2 cups cubed cooked chicken

½ can (10¾ ounces) condensed cream of chicken soup, undiluted

⅓ cup chopped slivered almonds, toasted

⅓ cup diced celery

⅓ cup diced red bell pepper

⅓ cup chopped fresh parsley

¼ cup diced onion

¼ cup chicken broth or white wine

2 tablespoons half-and-half (optional)

1. Bake pastry shells according to package directions. Keep warm.

2. Prepare rice according to package directions.

3. Add remaining ingredients to rice; mix well. Cook over medium heat 4 to 5 minutes or until bubbly and heated through. Fill pastry shells with rice mixture. Serve immediately.

Tip: This is a delicious way to use leftover chicken.

Spinach-Artichoke Party Cups

Spinach-Artichoke Party Cups

Makes 36 appetizers

Nonstick cooking spray
36 (3-inch) wonton
    wrappers
1 jar (about 6 ounces)
    marinated artichoke
    hearts, drained and
    chopped
½ (10-ounce) package
    frozen chopped
    spinach, thawed and
    squeezed dry
1 cup (4 ounces) shredded
    Monterey Jack cheese
½ cup grated Parmesan
    cheese
½ cup mayonnaise
1 clove garlic, minced

1. Preheat oven to 300°F. Spray mini (1¾-inch) muffin cups lightly with cooking spray. Press 1 wonton wrapper into each cup; spray lightly with cooking spray. Bake about 9 minutes or until light golden brown. Remove shells from pan; place on wire rack to cool. Repeat with remaining wonton wrappers.

2. Meanwhile, combine artichoke hearts, spinach, cheeses, mayonnaise and garlic in medium bowl; mix well.

3. Fill each wonton cup with about 1½ teaspoons spinach-artichoke mixture. Place filled cups on baking sheet. Bake about 7 minutes or until heated through. Serve immediately.

Tip: If you have leftover spinach-artichoke mixture after filling the wonton cups, place the mixture in a shallow ovenproof dish and bake it at 350°F until hot and bubbly. Serve it with bread or crackers as a dip.

Grilled Spiced Halibut, Pineapple and Pepper Skewers

Makes 6 servings

2 tablespoons lemon juice
  or lime juice
1 teaspoon minced garlic
1 teaspoon chili powder
½ teaspoon ground cumin
¼ teaspoon ground
  cinnamon
⅛ teaspoon ground cloves
½ pound boneless skinless
  halibut steak, about
  1 inch thick
½ small pineapple, peeled,
  halved lengthwise and
  cut into 24 pieces
1 large green or red bell
  pepper, cut into
  24 pieces

1. Combine lemon juice, garlic, chili powder, cumin, cinnamon and cloves in large resealable food storage bag; knead until blended.

2. Rinse fish; pat dry. Cut into 12 (1- to 1¼-inch) cubes. Add fish to bag. Press out air; seal. Turn gently to coat fish with marinade. Refrigerate 30 minutes to 1 hour. Soak 12 (6- to 8-inch) wooden skewers in water while fish marinates. Alternately thread 2 pieces pineapple, 2 pieces pepper and 1 piece fish onto each skewer.

3. Prepare grill for direct cooking. Spray grid with nonstick cooking spray. Place grid 4 to 6 inches above heat. Preheat grill to medium-high heat. Place skewers on grid. Cover or tent with foil; grill 3 to 4 minutes over medium-high heat or until grill marks appear on bottom. Turn skewers over; grill 3 to 4 minutes more or until fish begins to flake when tested with fork.

Sesame Chicken Salad Wonton Cups

Makes 10 servings

Nonstick cooking spray
20 (3-inch) wonton
    wrappers
1 tablespoon sesame seeds
2 boneless skinless
    chicken breasts (about
    8 ounces)
1 cup fresh green beans,
    cut diagonally into
    ½-inch pieces
¼ cup mayonnaise
1 tablespoon chopped
    fresh cilantro
    (optional)
2 teaspoons honey
1 teaspoon soy sauce
⅛ teaspoon ground red
    pepper

1. Preheat oven to 350°F. Spray mini (1¾-inch) muffin cups with cooking spray. Press 1 wonton wrapper into each muffin cup; spray with cooking spray. Bake 8 to 10 minutes or until golden brown. Cool in pan on wire rack before filling. Place sesame seeds in shallow baking pan. Bake 5 minutes or until lightly toasted, stirring occasionally. Set aside to cool.

2. Meanwhile, bring 2 cups water to a boil in medium saucepan. Add chicken. Reduce heat to low. Cover; simmer 10 minutes or until chicken is no longer pink in center, adding green beans after 7 minutes. Drain.

3. Finely chop chicken. Place in medium bowl. Add green beans and remaining ingredients; mix lightly. Spoon lightly rounded tablespoonful chicken mixture into each wonton cup. Garnish, if desired.

Pepper Cheese Cocktail Puffs

Pepper Cheese Cocktail Puffs

Makes about 20 appetizers

½ package (about 17 ounces) frozen puff pastry dough, thawed

1 tablespoon Dijon mustard

½ cup (2 ounces) finely shredded Cheddar cheese

1 teaspoon black pepper

1 egg

1 tablespoon water

1. Preheat oven to 400°F. Grease baking sheets.

2. Roll out 1 sheet of puff pastry on well-floured surface to 14×10-inch rectangle. Spread half of dough (from 10-inch side) with mustard. Sprinkle with cheese and pepper. Fold dough over filling; roll edges gently to seal. Cut lengthwise into 3 strips; cut each strip diagonally into 1½-inch pieces. Place on prepared baking sheets. Beat egg and water in small bowl; brush onto appetizers.

3. Bake appetizers 12 to 15 minutes or until puffed and deep golden brown. Remove from baking sheets to wire rack; cool.

Prep and Bake Time: 30 minutes

Tip: Work quickly and efficiently when using puff pastry. The colder puff pastry is, the better it will puff in the hot oven.

Mini Marinated Beef Skewers

Mini Marinated Beef Skewers

Makes 6 servings (3 skewers each)

1 beef top round steak
(about 1 pound)
2 tablespoons soy sauce
1 tablespoon dry sherry
1 teaspoon dark sesame oil
2 cloves garlic, minced
18 cherry tomatoes
(optional)

1. Preheat broiler. Cut beef crosswise into 18 (⅛-inch-thick) slices. Place in large resealable food storage bag. Combine soy sauce, sherry, oil and garlic in small cup; pour over beef. Seal bag; turn to coat. Marinate in refrigerator at least 30 minutes or up to 2 hours.

2. Meanwhile, soak 18 (6-inch) wooden skewers in water 20 minutes. Preheat broiler. Drain beef; discard marinade. Weave beef accordion-style onto skewers. Place on rack of broiler pan.

3. Broil 4 to 5 inches from heat 2 minutes. Turn skewers over; broil 2 minutes more or until beef is barely pink. Garnish each skewer with 1 cherry tomato. Serve warm.

Almond Chicken Cups

Makes 12 chicken cups

1 tablespoon vegetable oil
½ cup chopped onion
½ cup chopped red bell
    pepper
2 cups chopped cooked
    chicken
⅔ cup sweet and sour
    sauce
½ cup chopped almonds
2 tablespoons soy sauce
6 (6- to 7-inch) flour
    tortillas

1. Preheat oven to 400°F. Heat oil in small skillet over medium heat. Add onion and bell pepper. Cook and stir 3 minutes or until crisp-tender.

2. Combine vegetable mixture, chicken, sweet and sour sauce, almonds and soy sauce in medium bowl; mix until well blended.

3. Cut each tortilla in half. Place each half in standard (2¾-inch) muffin cup. Fill each with about ¼ cup chicken mixture. Bake 8 to 10 minutes or until tortilla edges are crisp and filling is heated through. Cool on wire rack 5 minutes before serving.

Prep and Cook Time: 30 minutes

Spinach Cheese Bundles

Spinach Cheese Bundles

Makes 32 bundles

1 package (6½ ounces) garlic-and-herb spreadable cheese
½ cup packed chopped spinach
¼ teaspoon black pepper
1 package (about 17 ounces) frozen puff pastry, thawed
Sweet and sour sauce (optional)

1. Preheat oven to 400°F. Combine cheese, spinach and pepper in small bowl; mix well.

2. Roll out each sheet of puff pastry into 12-inch square on lightly floured surface. Cut each square into 16 (3-inch) squares. Place about 1 teaspoon cheese mixture in center of each square. Brush edges of squares with water. Bring edges together over filling; twist tightly to seal. Fan out corners of puff pastry.

3. Place bundles 2 inches apart on ungreased baking sheets. Bake about 13 minutes or until golden brown. Serve warm with sweet and sour sauce, if desired.

Spicy Orange Chicken Kabob Appetizers

Makes 12 servings

2 boneless skinless
   chicken breasts
   (4 ounces each)
1 small red or green bell
   pepper
24 small button mushrooms
½ cup orange juice
2 tablespoons soy sauce
1 tablespoon vegetable oil
1½ teaspoons onion powder
½ teaspoon Chinese
   5-spice powder★

★Chinese 5-spice powder is a blend of cinnamon, star anise, fennel seed, anise and ginger. It is available in most supermarkets and at Asian grocery stores.

1. Cut chicken and bell pepper into 24 (¾-inch) square pieces. Place chicken, pepper and mushrooms in large resealable food storage bag. Combine orange juice, soy sauce, oil, onion powder and 5-spice powder in small bowl. Pour over chicken and vegetables. Seal bag; turn to coat. Marinate in refrigerator 4 to 24 hours, turning frequently.

2. Soak 24 small wooden skewers or toothpicks in water 20 minutes. Meanwhile, preheat broiler. Coat broiler pan with nonstick cooking spray.

3. Drain chicken mixture, reserving marinade. Thread 1 piece chicken, 1 piece pepper and 1 mushroom onto each skewer. Place on prepared pan. Brush with marinade; discard remaining marinade. Broil 4 inches from heat 5 to 6 minutes or until chicken is no longer pink in center. Serve immediately.

Egg Champignons

Makes 24 appetizers

6 eggs, hard cooked, peeled and chopped
¼ cup dry bread crumbs
¼ cup (1 ounce) crumbled blue cheese
2 tablespoons thinly sliced green onions
2 tablespoons dry white wine
2 tablespoons butter, melted
1 tablespoon chopped fresh parsley *or* 1½ teaspoons dried parsley flakes
½ teaspoon garlic salt
24 large mushroom caps (about 1½ inches in diameter)
Paprika (optional)
Green onions and tomato slices (optional)

1. Preheat oven to 450°F. Lightly grease baking sheet. Combine eggs, bread crumbs, blue cheese, 2 tablespoons green onions, wine, butter, parsley and garlic salt in medium bowl.

2. Fill each mushroom cap with 1 rounded tablespoonful egg mixture. Place mushroom caps on prepared baking sheet.

3. Bake 8 to 10 minutes. Sprinkle with paprika and garnish with green onions and tomato slices.

TOP THESE!

Pepperoni-Oregano Focaccia

Makes 12 servings

1 tablespoon cornmeal
1 package (about
    14 ounces)
    refrigerated pizza
    crust dough
½ cup finely chopped
    pepperoni (3 to
    3½ ounces)
1½ teaspoons finely
    chopped fresh oregano
    or ½ teaspoon dried
    oregano
2 teaspoons extra-virgin
    olive oil

1. Preheat oven to 425°F. Spray baking sheet with nonstick cooking spray; sprinkle with cornmeal. Set aside.

2. Unroll dough onto lightly floured surface. Pat dough into 12×9-inch rectangle. Sprinkle half the pepperoni and half the oregano over one side of dough. Fold over dough, making 12×4½-inch rectangle. Roll dough into 12×9-inch rectangle. Place on prepared baking sheet. Prick dough with fork at 2-inch intervals (about 30 times). Brush with oil; sprinkle with remaining pepperoni and oregano.

3. Bake 12 to 15 minutes or until golden brown. (Prick dough several more times if dough puffs as it bakes.) Cut into strips.

Tortilla Pizzettes

Makes about 30 servings

1 cup chunky salsa
1 cup refried beans
2 tablespoons chopped
  fresh cilantro
½ teaspoon ground cumin
3 (10-inch) flour tortillas
1 cup (4 ounces) shredded
  Mexican cheese blend

1. Pour salsa into strainer; let drain at least 20 minutes. Meanwhile, combine refried beans, cilantro and cumin in small bowl; mix well. Preheat oven to 400°F. Spray baking sheet lightly with nonstick cooking spray; set aside.

2. Cut each tortilla into 2½-inch circles using cookie cutter (9 to 10 circles per tortilla). Spread each tortilla circle with refried bean mixture, leaving ¼ inch around edge. Top each with heaping teaspoonful drained salsa; sprinkle with about 1½ teaspoons cheese.

3. Place tortillas on prepared baking sheet. Bake about 7 minutes or until tortillas are golden brown.

Chicken Pesto Pizza

Makes about 20 pieces

Cornmeal
1 loaf (1 pound) frozen
   bread dough, thawed
Nonstick cooking spray
8 ounces chicken tenders,
   cut into ½-inch
   pieces
½ red onion, cut into
   quarters and thinly
   sliced
¼ cup prepared pesto
2 large plum tomatoes,
   seeded and diced
1 cup (4 ounces) shredded
   pizza cheese blend or
   mozzarella cheese

1. Preheat oven to 375°F. Sprinkle baking sheet with cornmeal. Roll out bread dough on floured surface to 14×8-inch rectangle. Transfer to prepared baking sheet. Cover loosely with plastic wrap; let rise 20 to 30 minutes.

2. Meanwhile, spray large skillet with cooking spray. Add chicken; cook and stir over medium heat 2 minutes. Add onion and pesto; cook and stir 3 to 4 minutes or until chicken is cooked through. Stir in tomatoes. Remove from heat; let cool slightly.

3. Spread chicken mixture evenly over dough to within 1 inch of edges. Sprinkle with cheese. Bake on bottom rack of oven about 20 minutes or until crust is golden brown. Cut into 2-inch squares.

Mediterranean Flatbread

Makes about 16 pieces

2 tablespoons olive oil, divided
½ cup thinly sliced yellow onion
½ cup thinly sliced red bell pepper
½ cup thinly sliced green bell pepper
1 package (11 ounces) refrigerated French bread dough
2 cloves garlic, minced
½ teaspoon dried rosemary
⅛ teaspoon red pepper flakes (optional)
⅓ cup coarsely chopped pitted kalamata olives
¼ cup grated Parmesan cheese

1. Preheat oven to 350°F. Heat 1 tablespoon oil in large skillet over medium-high heat. Add onion and bell peppers; cook and stir 5 minutes or until onion begins to brown. Remove from heat.

2. Unroll dough on nonstick baking sheet. Combine garlic and remaining 1 tablespoon oil; spread evenly over dough. Sprinkle with rosemary and red pepper flakes, if desired. Top with onion mixture; sprinkle with olives.

3. Bake 16 to 18 minutes or until golden brown. Sprinkle with cheese. Cool on wire rack. Cut flatbread in half lengthwise; cut crosswise into 1-inch-wide strips.

Carpaccio di Zucchini

Makes 4 servings

12 ounces zucchini, shredded

½ cup sliced almonds, toasted

1 tablespoon Italian dressing

4 French rolls, cut in half lengthwise

1 tablespoon plus 1 teaspoon soft-spread margarine

3 tablespoons grated Parmesan cheese

Pear tomatoes, halved (optional)

1. Preheat broiler. Place zucchini in medium bowl. Add almonds and dressing; mix well. Set aside.

2. Place roll halves on baking sheet; spread evenly with margarine. Sprinkle with cheese. Broil 3 inches from heat 2 to 3 minutes or until edges and cheese are browned.

3. Spread zucchini mixture evenly onto each roll half. Garnish with tomatoes. Serve immediately.

SERVING SUGGESTION: Serve with spaghetti and tomato sauce.

Prep and Cook Time: 28 minutes

Shrimp Toast

Makes 2 dozen appetizers

½ pound raw shrimp, peeled and deveined
2 tablespoons chopped green onion
2 tablespoons finely chopped water chestnuts
2 tablespoons soy sauce
1 teaspoon dark sesame oil
1 egg white, lightly beaten
6 slices white sandwich bread, crusts removed
   Red and yellow bell pepper strips (optional)

1. Finely chop shrimp. If using food processor, process using on/off pulses about 10 times or until shrimp are finely chopped. Combine shrimp, onion, water chestnuts, soy sauce and sesame oil in medium bowl; mix well. Stir in egg white; mix well.★

2. Toast bread lightly on both sides. Cut diagonally into quarters. Spread shrimp mixture evenly over toast to edges.

3. Place toast on foil-lined baking sheet or broiler pan. Broil 6 inches from heat 4 minutes or until lightly browned. Garnish with peppers.

★The filling may be made ahead to this point. Cover and refrigerate filling up to 24 hours. Proceed as directed in step 3.

Venetian Canapés

Makes 24 appetizers

12 slices firm white bread
5 tablespoons butter or margarine, divided
2 tablespoons all-purpose flour
½ cup milk
3 ounces fresh mushrooms (about 9 medium), finely chopped
6 tablespoons grated Parmesan cheese, divided
2 teaspoons anchovy paste
¼ teaspoon salt
⅛ teaspoon black pepper
Green and black olive slices and red and green bell pepper strips (optional)

1. Preheat oven to 350°F. Cut 2 rounds out of each bread slice with 2-inch cookie cutter. Melt 3 tablespoons butter in small saucepan. Brush both sides of bread rounds lightly with butter. Bake bread rounds on ungreased baking sheet 5 to 6 minutes per side or until golden. Remove to wire rack. Cool completely. *Increase oven temperature to 425°F.*

2. Melt remaining 2 tablespoons butter in same saucepan. Stir in flour; cook and stir over medium heat until bubbly. Whisk in milk; cook and stir 1 minute or until sauce thickens and bubbles. (Sauce will be very thick.) Place mushrooms in large bowl; stir in sauce, 3 tablespoons cheese, anchovy paste, salt and black pepper until well blended.

3. Spread 1 heaping teaspoonful mushroom mixture onto each toast round; place on ungreased baking sheets. Sprinkle remaining 3 tablespoons cheese over rounds. Bake 5 to 7 minutes or until light brown. Garnish with olive slices and pepper strips.

Mediterranean Pita Pizzas

Mediterranean Pita Pizzas

Makes 8 servings

2 (8-inch) rounds pita bread
1 teaspoon olive oil
1 cup canned cannellini beans, rinsed and drained
2 teaspoons lemon juice
2 cloves garlic, minced
½ cup thinly sliced radicchio or escarole lettuce (optional)
½ cup chopped seeded tomato
½ cup finely chopped red onion
¼ cup (1 ounce) crumbled feta cheese
2 tablespoons sliced pitted black olives

1. Preheat oven to 450°F. Arrange pitas on baking sheet; brush tops with oil. Bake 6 minutes.

2. Meanwhile, place beans in small bowl; mash lightly with fork. Stir in lemon juice and garlic.

3. Spread bean mixture evenly on pita rounds to within ½ inch of edges. Top with radicchio, if desired, tomato, onion, feta and olives. Bake 5 minutes or until toppings are thoroughly heated and crust is crisp. Cut into wedges; serve hot.

TOP THESE!

Bruschetta

Makes 4 servings

Nonstick cooking spray
1 cup thinly sliced onion
½ cup chopped seeded
  tomato
2 tablespoons capers,
  drained
¼ teaspoon black pepper
3 cloves garlic, finely
  chopped
1 teaspoon olive oil
4 slices French bread
½ cup (2 ounces) shredded
  Monterey Jack cheese

1. Spray large nonstick skillet with cooking spray. Cook and stir onion over medium heat 5 minutes. Stir in tomato, capers and pepper. Cook 3 minutes.

2. Preheat broiler.

3. Combine garlic and olive oil in small bowl. Brush bread slices with oil mixture. Top with onion mixture; sprinkle with cheese. Place on baking sheet. Broil 3 minutes or until cheese melts.

Tip: Before using capers, be sure to thoroughly rinse them with water and blot with a paper towel.

Fast Pesto Focaccia

Makes 16 servings

1 can (about 13 ounces) refrigerated pizza dough
2 tablespoons prepared pesto
4 sun-dried tomatoes, packed in oil, drained

1. Preheat oven to 425°F. Lightly grease 8-inch square baking pan. Unroll pizza dough. Fold in half; press gently into pan.

2. Spread pesto evenly over dough. Chop tomatoes or snip with kitchen scissors; sprinkle over pesto. Press tomatoes into dough. Using wooden spoon handle, make indentations in dough every 2 inches.

3. Bake 10 to 12 minutes or until golden brown. Cut into 16 squares. Serve warm or at room temperature.

Prep and Cook Time: 20 minutes

WINGS & THINGS

Jerk Wings with Ranch Dipping Sauce

Makes 6 to 7 servings

½ cup mayonnaise
½ cup plain yogurt or sour cream
1½ teaspoons salt, divided
1¼ teaspoons garlic powder, divided
½ teaspoon black pepper, divided
¼ teaspoon onion powder
2 tablespoons orange juice
1 teaspoon sugar
1 teaspoon dried thyme leaves
1 teaspoon paprika
¼ teaspoon ground nutmeg
¼ teaspoon ground red pepper
2½ pounds chicken wings (about 10 wings)

1. Preheat oven to 450°F. For dipping sauce, combine mayonnaise, yogurt, ½ teaspoon salt, ¼ teaspoon garlic powder, ¼ teaspoon black pepper and onion powder in small bowl. Set aside.

2. Combine orange juice, sugar, thyme, paprika, nutmeg, red pepper and remaining 1 teaspoon salt, 1 teaspoon garlic powder and ¼ teaspoon black pepper in small bowl.

3. Cut tips from wings; discard. Place wings in large bowl. Drizzle with orange juice mixture; toss to coat. Transfer chicken to greased broiler pan. Bake 25 to 30 minutes or until juices run clear and skin is crisp. Serve with dipping sauce.

SERVING SUGGESTION:
Serve with celery sticks and/or deviled eggs.

Nicole's Cheddar Crisps

Nicole's Cheddar Crisps

Makes 32 crisps

1¾ cups all-purpose flour
½ cup yellow cornmeal
¾ teaspoon sugar
¾ teaspoon salt
½ teaspoon baking soda
½ cup (1 stick) butter or
    margarine
1½ cups (6 ounces)
    shredded sharp
    Cheddar cheese
½ cup cold water
2 tablespoons white
    vinegar
Black pepper

1. Combine flour, cornmeal, sugar, salt and baking soda in large bowl. Cut in butter with pastry blender or two knives until mixture resembles coarse crumbs. Stir in cheese, water and vinegar with fork until mixture forms soft dough. Cover dough; refrigerate 1 hour or freeze 30 minutes or until firm.

2. Preheat oven to 375°F. Grease 2 baking sheets. Divide dough into 4 pieces.★ Roll each piece into paper-thin circle, about 13 inches in diameter, on floured surface. Sprinkle with pepper; press pepper firmly into dough.

3. Cut each circle into 8 wedges; place on prepared baking sheets. Bake about 10 minutes or until crisp. Store in airtight container for up to 3 days.

★To prepare frozen dough, thaw in the refrigerator before proceeding as directed.

Buffalo Chicken Tenders

Buffalo Chicken Tenders

Makes 10 servings

3 tablespoons Louisiana-
style hot sauce
½ teaspoon paprika
¼ teaspoon ground red
pepper
1 pound chicken tenders
½ cup blue cheese dressing
¼ cup sour cream
2 tablespoons crumbled
blue cheese
1 medium green or red
bell pepper, cut
lengthwise into
½-inch-thick slices

1. Preheat oven to 375°F. Combine hot sauce, paprika and ground red pepper in small bowl; brush on all surfaces of chicken. Place chicken in greased 11×7-inch baking dish. Cover; marinate in refrigerator 30 minutes.

2. Bake, uncovered, about 15 minutes or until chicken is no longer pink in center.

3. Combine blue cheese dressing, sour cream and blue cheese in small serving bowl. Serve dip with chicken and pepper slices.

Spanish Omelet

Makes 6 servings

8 large eggs, beaten
3 cups (16 ounces) frozen
cubed or shredded
hash brown potatoes
1½ cups *French's*® French
Fried Onions
Salsa
Frank's® *RedHot*®
Original Cayenne
Pepper Sauce

1. Beat eggs with *½ teaspoon salt* and *¼ teaspoon pepper* in large bowl; set aside.

2. Heat *2 tablespoons oil* until very hot in 10-inch nonstick oven–safe skillet over medium–high heat. Sauté potatoes about 7 minutes or until browned, stirring often.

3. Stir *½ cup* French Fried Onions and beaten eggs into potato mixture. Cook, uncovered, over low heat 15 minutes or until eggs are almost set. *Do not stir.* Sprinkle eggs with remaining *1 cup* onions. Cover and cook 8 minutes or until eggs are fully set. Cut into wedges and serve with salsa. Splash on *Frank's RedHot* Sauce to taste.

Prep Time: 5 minutes
Cook Time: 30 minutes

One Potato, Two Potato

Makes 4 servings

Nonstick cooking spray
2 medium baking potatoes, cut lengthwise into 4 wedges
Salt (optional)
½ cup plain dry bread crumbs
2 tablespoons grated Parmesan cheese (optional)
1½ teaspoons dried oregano, dill weed, Italian seasoning or paprika
Spicy brown or honey mustard, ketchup or sour cream (optional)

1. Preheat oven to 425°F. Spray baking sheet with cooking spray; set aside.

2. Spray cut sides of potatoes generously with cooking spray; sprinkle lightly with salt, if desired.

3. Combine bread crumbs, Parmesan cheese, if desired and oregano in shallow dish. Add potatoes; toss lightly until potatoes are generously coated with crumb mixture. Place on prepared baking sheet. Bake potatoes about 20 minutes or until potatoes are brown and tender. Serve warm with mustard for dipping, if desired.

POTATO SWEETS:
Omit bread crumbs, Parmesan cheese, oregano and mustard. Substitute sweet potatoes for baking potatoes. Cut and spray potatoes as directed; coat generously with desired amount of cinnamon-sugar. Bake as directed. Serve warm with peach or pineapple preserves or honey mustard for dipping. Makes 4 servings.

Angel Wings

Angel Wings

Makes 4 servings

1 can (10¾ ounces)
    condensed tomato
    soup, undiluted
¾ cup water
¼ cup packed brown sugar
2½ tablespoons balsamic
    vinegar
2 tablespoons chopped
    shallots
12 chicken wings

SLOW COOKER DIRECTIONS

1. Combine soup, water, brown sugar, vinegar and shallots in slow cooker; mix well.

2. Add chicken wings; stir to coat with sauce.

3. Cover; cook on LOW 5 to 6 hours or until cooked through.

Tip: To make cleanup easier, spray the inside of the slow cooker with nonstick cooking spray before adding the ingredients.

Herbed Potato Chips

Herbed Potato Chips

Makes 6 servings

Nonstick olive oil
  cooking spray
2 medium red potatoes
  (about ½ pound),
  unpeeled
1 tablespoon olive oil
2 tablespoons minced
  fresh dill, thyme or
  rosemary leaves *or*
  2 teaspoons dried
  dill weed, thyme or
  rosemary
¼ teaspoon garlic salt
⅛ teaspoon black pepper
1¼ cups sour cream

1. Preheat oven to 450°F. Spray baking sheets with cooking spray.

2. Cut potatoes crosswise into very thin slices, about 1/16 inch thick. Pat dry with paper towels. Arrange potato slices in single layer on prepared baking sheets; coat potatoes with cooking spray.

3. Bake 10 minutes; turn slices over. Brush with oil. Combine dill, garlic salt and pepper in small bowl; sprinkle evenly onto potato slices. Continue baking 5 to 10 minutes or until potatoes are golden brown. Cool on baking sheets. Serve with sour cream.

Barbecued Ribs

Makes 8 servings

3 to 4 pounds lean pork
  baby back ribs or
  spareribs
⅓ cup hoisin sauce
4 tablespoons soy sauce,
  divided
3 tablespoons dry sherry
3 cloves garlic, minced
2 tablespoons honey
1 tablespoon dark sesame
  oil

1. Place ribs in large resealable food storage bag. Combine hoisin sauce, 3 tablespoons soy sauce, sherry and garlic in small cup; pour over ribs. Seal bag; turn to coat. Marinate in refrigerator at least 4 hours or up to 24 hours.

2. Preheat oven to 375°F. Drain ribs; reserve marinade. Place ribs on rack in shallow, foil-lined roasting pan. Bake 30 minutes. Turn; brush ribs with half of reserved marinade. Bake 15 minutes. Turn ribs over; brush with remaining marinade. Bake 15 minutes.

3. Combine remaining 1 tablespoon soy sauce, honey and sesame oil in small bowl; brush over ribs. Bake 5 to 10 minutes or until ribs are cooked through, browned and crisp.★ Cut into serving pieces.

★Ribs may be made ahead to this point. Cover and refrigerate up to 3 days. To reheat, wrap ribs in foil; cook in preheated 350°F oven 30 minutes or until heated through. Cut into serving pieces.

Baked Garlic Bundles

Baked Garlic Bundles

Makes 2 dozen appetizers

½ (16-ounce) package frozen phyllo dough, thawed to room temperature

¾ cup (1½ sticks) butter, melted

3 large heads garlic,★ separated into cloves and peeled

½ cup finely chopped walnuts

1 cup Italian-style bread crumbs

★The whole garlic bulb is called a head.

1. Preheat oven to 350°F. Remove phyllo from package; unroll and place on large sheet of waxed paper. Using scissors, cut phyllo crosswise into 2-inch-wide strips. Cover with large sheet of waxed paper and damp kitchen towel. (Phyllo dries out quickly if not covered.)

2. Lay 1 phyllo strip on flat surface; brush immediately with melted butter. Place 1 clove garlic at end of strip. Sprinkle about 1 teaspoon walnuts over length of strip. Roll up garlic clove and walnuts in phyllo strip, tucking in side edges while rolling. Brush bundle with melted butter; roll in bread crumbs to coat. Repeat with remaining phyllo strips, garlic cloves, walnuts, butter and bread crumbs until all but smallest garlic cloves are used.

3. Place bundles on rack in shallow roasting pan. Bake 20 minutes or until crispy.

Can't Get Enough Chicken Wings

Makes 36 appetizers

18 chicken wings (about 3 pounds)
1 envelope LIPTON® RECIPE SECRETS® Savory Herb with Garlic Soup Mix
½ cup water
2 to 3 tablespoons hot pepper sauce★ (optional)
2 tablespoons margarine or butter

★Use more or less hot pepper sauce as desired.

1. Cut tips off chicken wings (save tips for soup). Cut chicken wings in half at joint. Deep fry, bake or broil until golden brown and crunchy.

2. Meanwhile, in small saucepan, combine soup mix, water and hot pepper sauce. Cook over low heat, stirring occasionally, 2 minutes or until thickened. Remove from heat and stir in margarine.

3. In large bowl, toss cooked chicken wings with hot soup mixture until evenly coated. Serve, if desired, over greens with cut-up celery.

DIPS & SPREADS

Summer Fruits with Peanut Butter-Honey Dip

Makes 4 servings (about ½ cup dip)

⅓ cup peanut butter
2 tablespoons milk
2 tablespoons honey
1 tablespoon apple juice
    or water
⅛ teaspoon ground
    cinnamon
2 cups melon balls,
    including cantaloupe
    and honeydew
1 peach or nectarine,
    pitted and cut into
    8 wedges
1 banana, peeled and
    thickly sliced

1. Place peanut butter in small bowl; gradually stir in milk and honey until blended.

2. Stir in apple juice and cinnamon until mixture is smooth.

3. Serve dip with prepared fruits.

Prep Time: 20 minutes

Roasted Garlic Hummus

Makes 6 servings

2 tablespoons Roasted
  Garlic (recipe follows)
1 can (15 ounces)
  chickpeas, rinsed and
  drained
¼ cup fresh parsley sprigs
2 tablespoons water
2 tablespoons lemon juice
½ teaspoon curry powder
⅛ teaspoon dark sesame oil
  Dash hot pepper sauce
  (optional)
  Pita bread wedges and
  fresh vegetables

1. Prepare Roasted Garlic.

2. Place chickpeas, parsley,
2 tablespoons Roasted Garlic, water,
lemon juice, curry powder, sesame
oil and hot pepper sauce, if desired,
in food processor or blender. Cover;
process until smooth.

3. Serve with pita wedges and
vegetables.

ROASTED GARLIC:
Cut off top third of 1 large garlic
head (not the root end) to expose
cloves; discard top. Place head of
garlic, trimmed end up, on 10-inch
square of foil. Rub garlic generously
with olive oil and sprinkle with salt.
Gather foil ends together and close
tightly. Roast in preheated 350°F
oven 45 minutes or until cloves are
golden and soft. When cool enough
to handle, squeeze roasted garlic
cloves from skins; discard skins.

Nutty Bacon Cheeseball

Nutty Bacon Cheeseball

Makes about 24 servings

1 package (8 ounces)
   cream cheese, softened
½ cup milk
2 cups (8 ounces)
   shredded sharp
   Cheddar cheese
2 cups (8 ounces)
   shredded Monterey
   Jack cheese
¼ cup (1 ounce) crumbled
   blue cheese
10 slices bacon, cooked,
   crumbled and divided
¾ cup finely chopped
   pecans, divided
¼ cup finely minced green
   onions (white parts
   only)
1 jar (2 ounces) diced
   pimiento, drained
   Salt and black pepper
¼ cup minced fresh
   parsley
1 tablespoon poppy seeds

1. Beat cream cheese and milk in large bowl with electric mixer at low speed until blended. Add Cheddar cheese, Monterey Jack cheese and blue cheese; beat at medium speed until well mixed. Add half of bacon, half of pecans, green onions and pimiento. Beat at medium speed until well mixed. Add salt and pepper to taste.

2. Transfer half of mixture to large piece of plastic wrap. Shape into ball; wrap tightly. Repeat with remaining mixture. Refrigerate at least 2 hours or until chilled.

3. Combine remaining bacon, pecans, parsley and poppy seeds in pie plate. Remove plastic wrap from chilled cheese balls. Roll each in bacon mixture until well coated. Wrap ball tightly in plastic wrap; refrigerate up to 24 hours.

Roasted Eggplant Spread

Makes 4 servings

1 large eggplant
1 can (about 14 ounces)
  diced tomatoes,
  drained
½ cup finely chopped
  green onions
½ cup chopped fresh
  parsley
2 tablespoons red wine
  vinegar
1 tablespoon olive oil
3 cloves garlic, finely
  chopped
½ teaspoon salt
½ teaspoon dried oregano
2 (8-inch) rounds pita
  bread
  Fresh lemon or lime
  wedges (optional)

1. Preheat oven to 375°F. Place eggplant on baking sheet. Bake 1 hour or until tender, turning occasionally. Remove eggplant from oven. Let stand 10 minutes or until cool enough to handle.

2. Cut eggplant in half lengthwise; remove pulp. Discard stem and skin. Place pulp in medium bowl; mash with fork until smooth. Add tomatoes, green onions, parsley, vinegar, oil, garlic, salt and oregano; blend well. Cover eggplant mixture; refrigerate 2 hours.

3. Preheat broiler. Split pita breads horizontally in half to form 4 rounds. Stack pita rounds; cut into sixths to form 24 wedges. Place wedges on baking sheet. Broil 4 inches from heat 3 minutes or until crisp. Serve eggplant spread with warm pita wedges. Garnish with lemons.

Chutney Cheese Spread

Makes about 20 servings

2 packages (8 ounces each) cream cheese, softened
1 cup (4 ounces) shredded Cheddar cheese
½ cup mango chutney
¼ cup sliced green onions
3 tablespoons dark raisins, chopped
2 cloves garlic, minced
1 to 1½ teaspoons curry powder
¾ teaspoon ground coriander
½ to ¾ teaspoon ground ginger
1 tablespoon chopped dry-roasted peanuts
Toasted bread slices

1. Place cream cheese and Cheddar cheese in food processor or blender; process until smooth.

2. Stir in chutney, green onions, raisins, garlic, curry powder, coriander and ginger. Cover; refrigerate 2 to 3 hours.

3. Sprinkle peanuts over spread just before serving. Serve with toasted bread slices.

VARIATION:
Try substituting 1 tablespoon toasted coconut for the peanuts in this recipe to give it a slightly sweeter flavor.

Roasted Garlic Spread with Three Cheeses

Makes about 20 servings

2 medium heads garlic
2 packages (8 ounces each) cream cheese, softened
1 package (3½ ounces) goat cheese
2 tablespoons (1 ounce) crumbled blue cheese
1 teaspoon dried thyme
Assorted sliced fresh vegetables
Fresh thyme and red bell pepper (optional)

1. Preheat oven to 400°F. Cut tops off garlic heads to expose tops of cloves. Place garlic in small baking pan. Bake 45 minutes or until very tender. Remove from pan; cool completely. Squeeze garlic into small bowl; mash with fork. Discard skins.

2. Beat cream cheese and goat cheese in small bowl until smooth; stir in garlic, blue cheese and thyme. Cover; refrigerate 3 hours or overnight.

3. Spoon dip into serving bowl; serve with fresh vegetables. Garnish with thyme and bell pepper.

Honey-Nut Glazed Brie

Makes 8 servings

8 ounces Brie cheese
(wedge or round)
¼ cup I CAN'T
BELIEVE IT'S NOT
BUTTER!® Spread
1 cup coarsely chopped
walnuts
¼ teaspoon ground
cinnamon (optional)
⅛ teaspoon ground
nutmeg (optional)
2 tablespoons honey
2 large green and/or red
apples, cored and
thinly sliced

Arrange cheese on serving platter; set aside.★

In 10-inch nonstick skillet, melt I Can't Believe It's Not Butter!® Spread over medium-high heat and stir in walnuts until coated.

Stir in cinnamon and nutmeg until blended. Stir in honey and cook, stirring constantly, 2 minutes or until mixture is bubbling. Immediately pour over cheese. Serve hot with apples.

★You may arrange cheese on microwave-safe plate and top with cooked nut mixture. Microwave at HIGH (Full Power) 1 minute or until cheese is warm. OR, in 1-quart shallow casserole, arrange cheese and top with cooked nut mixture. Bake at 350°F for 10 minutes or until Brie just begins to melt. Serve as above.

Party Cheese Spread

Makes about 2 cups spread

1 cup ricotta cheese
6 ounces cream cheese, softened
1 medium onion, chopped
2 tablespoons grated Parmesan cheese
1 tablespoon drained capers
2 anchovy fillets, mashed *or* 2 teaspoons anchovy paste
1 teaspoon dry mustard
1 teaspoon paprika
½ teaspoon hot pepper sauce
   Red cabbage or bell pepper

1. Beat ricotta cheese and cream cheese in large bowl with electric mixer on medium speed 3 to 5 minutes or until well blended. Stir in onion, Parmesan cheese, capers, anchovies, mustard, paprika and hot pepper sauce; mix well. Cover; refrigerate at least 1 day or up to 1 week to allow flavors to blend.

2. Just before serving, remove and discard any damaged outer leaves from cabbage. Slice small piece from bottom, so cabbage will sit flat. Cut out and remove inside portion of cabbage, leaving 1-inch-thick shell, being careful not to cut through bottom of cabbage.

3. Spoon cheese spread into hollowed-out cabbage. Serve with crackers and raw vegetables. Garnish as desired.

Seafood Spread

Makes 12 servings (1½ cups)

1 package (8 ounces)
    cream cheese,
    softened
½ pound smoked
    whitefish, skinned,
    boned and flaked
2 tablespoons minced
    green onion
1 tablespoon plus
    1 teaspoon chopped
    fresh dill
1 teaspoon lemon juice
¼ teaspoon black pepper
    Rye bread halves
    Lime wedges (optional)

1. Beat cream cheese in medium bowl with electric mixer at medium speed 2 to 3 minutes or until smooth. Add whitefish, green onion, dill, lemon juice and pepper; mix until well blended.

2. Refrigerate until ready to serve.

3. Serve with rye bread and garnish with lime wedges.

Prep Time: 10 minutes

Nutty Carrot Spread

Makes 18 servings

¼ cup finely chopped pecans

6 ounces cream cheese, softened

2 tablespoons frozen orange juice concentrate, thawed

¼ teaspoon ground cinnamon

1 cup shredded carrots

¼ cup raisins

36 slices toasted party pumpernickel bread or melba toast rounds

1. Preheat oven to 350°F. Place pecans in shallow baking pan. Bake 6 to 8 minutes or until lightly toasted, stirring occasionally. Cool slightly.

2. Meanwhile, combine cream cheese, juice concentrate and cinnamon in small bowl; stir until well blended. Stir in carrots, pecans and raisins.

3. Serve spread with bread or melba toast.

MEXICAN FIESTA

Tuna Quesadilla Stack

Makes 4 servings

4 (10-inch) flour tortillas
¼ cup plus 2 tablespoons pinto or black bean dip
1 can (about 14 ounces) diced tomatoes, drained
1 can (9 ounces) tuna packed in water, drained and flaked
2 cups (8 ounces) shredded Cheddar cheese
½ cup thinly sliced green onions
1½ teaspoons butter or margarine, melted

1. Preheat oven to 400°F.

2. Place 1 tortilla on 12-inch pizza pan. Spread with 2 tablespoons bean dip, leaving ½-inch border. Top with one third each of tomatoes, tuna, cheese and green onions. Repeat layers twice, beginning with tortilla and ending with onions. Top with remaining tortilla, pressing gently. Brush with melted butter.

3. Bake 15 minutes or until cheese melts and top is lightly browned. Cool slightly. Cut into 8 wedges.

Prep and Cook Time: 25 minutes

Tip: For a special touch, serve with assorted toppings such as guacamole, sour cream and salsa.

Nachos con Queso y Cerveza

Makes 4 servings

24 tortilla chips (about 4 ounces)

Nonstick cooking spray

¾ cup chopped red onion

2 jalapeño peppers,★ seeded and chopped

3 cloves garlic, finely chopped

2 teaspoons chili powder

½ teaspoon ground cumin

2 boneless skinless chicken breasts (about 8 ounces), cooked and chopped

1 can (about 14 ounces) Mexican-style diced tomatoes, drained

⅓ cup pilsner lager

1 cup (4 ounces) shredded Monterey Jack cheese

2 tablespoons chopped black olives

★Jalapeño peppers can sting and irritate the skin, so wear rubber gloves when handling peppers and do not touch your eyes.

1. Preheat oven to 350°F. Place chips in 13×9-inch baking pan; set aside.

2. Spray large nonstick skillet with cooking spray. Heat over medium heat. Add onion, jalapeños, garlic, chili powder and cumin. Cook 5 minutes or until vegetables are tender, stirring occasionally. Stir in chicken, tomatoes and lager. Simmer until liquid is absorbed.

3. Spoon chicken-tomato mixture over chips; top with cheese and olives. Bake 5 minutes or until cheese melts. Serve immediately.

Tex-Mex Potato Skins

Makes 18 servings

3 hot baked potatoes, split lengthwise
¾ cup (3 ounces) shredded Cheddar or pepper Jack cheese
1⅓ cups *French's*® French Fried Onions, divided
¼ cup chopped green chilies
¼ cup crumbled cooked bacon
Salsa and sour cream

1. Preheat oven to 350°F. Scoop out inside of potatoes, leaving ¼-inch shells. Reserve inside of potatoes for another use.

2. Arrange potato halves on baking sheet. Top with cheese, ⅔ *cup* French Fried Onions, chilies and bacon.

3. Bake 15 minutes or until heated through and cheese is melted. Cut each potato half crosswise into thirds. Serve topped with salsa, sour cream and remaining onions.

VARIATION:
For added Cheddar flavor, substitute *French's*® Cheddar French Fried Onions for the original flavor.

Prep Time: 15 minutes
Cook Time: 15 minutes

Tip: To bake potatoes quickly, microwave at HIGH 10 to 12 minutes or until tender.

Hearty Ham Quesadillas

Makes 8 servings

1 pound HILLSHIRE
FARM® Ham,
chopped
1 cup Monterey Jack
cheese
¼ cup minced onion
1 to 2 jalapeño peppers,★
seeded and minced
¼ cup minced cilantro
½ teaspoon black pepper
¼ teaspoon salt
8 (10-inch) flour tortillas
Prepared tomato salsa

★Jalapeño peppers can sting and
irritate the skin, so wear rubber
gloves when handling peppers and
do not touch your eyes.

Preheat oven to 500°F.

Combine Ham, cheese, onion,
jalapeño peppers, cilantro, black
pepper and salt in large bowl. Arrange
⅛ of ham mixture on each tortilla,
covering ½ of tortilla. Fold each
tortilla over to make half-moons.

Place tortillas in shallow baking pan.
Bake until tortillas are crisp and
golden, about 5 minutes. Cut into
wedges; serve with salsa.

Fiesta Chicken Nachos

Fiesta Chicken Nachos

Makes 4 servings

1 tablespoon olive oil
1 pound boneless, skinless chicken breasts
1 jar (1 pound) RAGÚ® Cheesy! Double Cheddar Sauce
1 bag (9 ounces) tortilla chips
2 green and/or red bell peppers, diced
1 small onion, chopped
1 large tomato, diced

1. In 12-inch skillet, heat olive oil over medium-high heat; cook chicken, turning occasionally, 8 minutes or until thoroughly cooked. Remove from skillet; cut into strips.

2. In same skillet, combine chicken and Ragú Cheesy! Double Cheddar Sauce; heat through.

3. On serving platter, arrange layer of tortilla chips, then ½ of the sauce mixture, bell peppers, onion and tomato; repeat, ending with tomato. Garnish, if desired, with chopped fresh cilantro and shredded lettuce.

Fast Guacamole and "Chips"

Makes 8 servings

2 ripe avocados
½ cup chunky salsa
¼ teaspoon hot pepper
 sauce (optional)
½ seedless cucumber,
 sliced into ⅛-inch-
 thick rounds

1. Cut avocados in half; remove and discard pits. Scoop flesh into medium bowl; mash with fork.

2. Add salsa and hot pepper sauce, if desired; mix well.

3. Transfer guacamole to serving bowl. Serve with cucumber "chips."

Tip: To prepare an avocado, insert a utility knife into the stem end. Slice in half lengthwise to the pit, turning the avocado while slicing. Remove the knife blade and twist the halves in opposite directions to pull apart.

Mexican Flats

Makes 2 servings

2 (6-inch) corn tortillas
½ cup (2 ounces) shredded sharp Cheddar cheese
2 tablespoons sour cream
¼ cup canned black beans, rinsed and drained
¼ cup salsa
¼ cup sliced black olives

1. Place 1 tortilla on each of 2 microwavable plates. Sprinkle ¼ cup cheese over each tortilla.

2. Cover each plate with waxed paper; microwave on HIGH 20 to 30 seconds or until cheese melts.

3. Carefully remove waxed paper. Spread 1 tablespoon sour cream over each tortilla. Top with black beans. Lightly mash beans with fork. Top each flat with salsa and olives. Serve open-faced or fold in half.

Nachos à la Ortega®

Makes 4 to 6 servings

1 can (16 ounces)
ORTEGA® Refried
Beans, warmed
4 cups baked tortilla chips
1½ cups (6 ounces)
shredded Monterey
Jack cheese
2 tablespoons ORTEGA®
Jalapeños, sliced

SUGGESTED TOPPINGS
ORTEGA® Salsa-Thick
& Chunky, sour
cream, guacamole,
sliced ripe olives,
chopped green
onions, chopped fresh
cilantro (optional)

PREHEAT broiler.

SPREAD beans over bottom
of large ovenproof platter or
15×10-inch jelly-roll pan. Arrange
chips over beans. Top with cheese and
jalapeños.

BROIL for 1 to 1½ minutes or until
cheese is melted. Top with desired
toppings.

Bite Size Tacos

Makes 8 servings

1 pound ground beef
1 package (1.25 ounces) taco seasoning mix
2 cups *French's*® French Fried Onions
¼ cup chopped fresh cilantro
32 bite-size round tortilla chips
¾ cup sour cream
1 cup (4 ounces) shredded Cheddar cheese

1. Cook beef in nonstick skillet over medium-high heat 5 minutes or until browned; drain. Stir in taco seasoning mix, *¾ cup water, 1 cup* French Fried Onions and cilantro. Simmer 5 minutes or until flavors are blended, stirring often.

2. Preheat oven to 350°F. Arrange tortilla chips on foil-lined baking sheet. Top with beef mixture, sour cream, remaining onions and cheese.

3. Bake 5 minutes or until cheese is melted and onions are golden.

Prep Time: 5 minutes
Cook Time: 15 minutes

Hearty Nachos

Makes 8 servings

1 pound ground beef
1 envelope LIPTON®
   RECIPE SECRETS®
   Onion Soup Mix
1 can (19 ounces) black
   beans, rinsed and
   drained
1 cup salsa
1 package (8½ ounces)
   plain tortilla chips
1 cup shredded Cheddar
   cheese (about
   4 ounces)

1. In 12-inch nonstick skillet, brown ground beef over medium-high heat; drain.

2. Stir in soup mix, black beans and salsa. Bring to a boil over high heat. Reduce heat to low and simmer 5 minutes or until heated through.

3. Arrange tortilla chips on serving platter. Spread beef mixture over chips; sprinkle with Cheddar cheese. Top, if desired, with sliced green onions, sliced pitted ripe olives, chopped tomato and chopped cilantro.

Prep Time: 10 minutes
Cook Time: 12 minutes

FESTIVE HOLIDAYS

Barbecued Meatballs

Makes about 4 dozen meatballs

2 pounds ground beef
1⅓ cups ketchup, divided
3 tablespoons seasoned
   dry bread crumbs
1 egg, lightly beaten
2 tablespoons dried onion
   flakes
¾ teaspoon garlic salt
½ teaspoon black pepper
1 cup packed light brown
   sugar
1 can (6 ounces) tomato
   paste
¼ cup soy sauce
¼ cup cider vinegar
1½ teaspoons hot pepper
   sauce
   Diced bell peppers
   (optional)

SLOW COOKER DIRECTIONS

1. Preheat oven to 350°F. Combine ground beef, ⅓ cup ketchup, bread crumbs, egg, onion flakes, garlic salt and black pepper in medium bowl. Mix lightly but thoroughly; shape into 1-inch meatballs.

2. Place meatballs in 2 (15×10-inch) jelly-roll pans or shallow roasting pans. Bake 18 minutes or until browned. Transfer meatballs to slow cooker.

3. Mix remaining 1 cup ketchup, sugar, tomato paste, soy sauce, vinegar and hot pepper sauce in medium bowl. Pour over meatballs. Cover; cook on LOW 4 hours. Serve with cocktail picks. Garnish with bell peppers, if desired.

BARBECUED FRANKS:
Arrange 2 (12-ounce) packages or 3 (8-ounce) packages cocktail franks in slow cooker. Combine 1 cup ketchup with brown sugar, tomato paste, soy sauce, vinegar and hot pepper sauce in medium bowl; pour over franks. Cook according to directions for Barbecued Meatballs.

Cheesy Christmas Trees

Makes about 12 appetizers

½ cup mayonnaise
1 tablespoon dry ranch
  salad dressing mix
1 cup (4 ounces) shredded
  Cheddar cheese
¼ cup grated Parmesan
  cheese
12 slices firm white bread
¼ cup red bell pepper
  strips
¼ cup green bell pepper
  strips

1. Preheat broiler. Combine mayonnaise and salad dressing mix in medium bowl. Add cheeses; mix well.

2. Cut bread slices into Christmas tree shapes with cookie cutter. Spread about 1 tablespoon mayonnaise mixture over each tree. Decorate with bell pepper strips. Place on baking sheet.

3. Broil 4 inches from heat 2 to 3 minutes or until bubbly. Serve warm.

Tip: Get creative with the Christmas tree decorating! Try different colored peppercorns for ornaments or sprinkle with chopped fresh parsley for more of an evergreen look.

Festive Taco Cups

Makes 36 taco cups

1 tablespoon vegetable oil
½ cup chopped onion
½ pound ground turkey or ground beef
1 clove garlic, minced
½ teaspoon dried oregano leaves
½ teaspoon chili powder or taco seasoning
¼ teaspoon salt
1¼ cups (5 ounces) shredded taco cheese or Mexican cheese blend, divided
1 can (11½ ounces) refrigerated corn breadstick dough
Chopped fresh tomato and sliced green onion (optional)

1. Heat oil in large skillet over medium heat. Add onion; cook until tender. Add turkey; cook until turkey is no longer pink, stirring occasionally. Stir in garlic, oregano, chili powder and salt. Remove from heat and stir in ½ cup cheese; set aside.

2. Preheat oven to 375°F. Lightly grease 36 mini (1¾-inch) muffin cups. Remove dough from container but do not unroll dough. Separate dough into 8 pieces at perforations. Divide each piece into 3 pieces; roll or pat each piece into 3-inch circle. Press circles into prepared muffin cups.

3. Fill each cup with 1½ to 2 teaspoons turkey mixture. Bake 10 minutes. Sprinkle tops of taco cups with remaining ¾ cup cheese; bake 2 to 3 minutes more or until cheese is melted. Garnish with tomato and green onion.

Gargoyle Tongues

Gargoyle Tongues

Makes 16 wedges

4 soft corn or flour tortillas
½ teaspoon ground cumin
1 cup (4 ounces) finely
shredded sharp
Cheddar
⅛ cup chopped ripe olives
3 tablespoons salsa

1. Preheat oven to 450°F. Sprinkle cumin evenly over tortillas and rub gently to lightly coat tortillas. Cut each tortilla into 4 wedges.

2. Coat nonstick baking sheet with cooking spray. Arrange wedges ½-inch apart on baking sheet; sprinkle evenly with cheese and olives. Bake 4 minutes or until cheese is melted.

3. Top each wedge with about ½ teaspoon of salsa in center and place on serving tray or large platter. *Do not stack wedges.*

Holiday Appetizer Puffs

Makes about 1½ dozen appetizers

1 sheet frozen puff pastry, thawed (half of 17¼-ounce package)
2 tablespoons olive or vegetable oil
Toppings: grated Parmesan cheese, sesame seeds, poppy seeds, dried dill weed, dried basil, paprika, drained capers or pimiento-stuffed green olive slices

1. Preheat oven to 425°F. Roll out pastry on lightly floured surface into 13-inch square. Cut out shapes with cookie cutters. (Simple shapes work best.) Place on ungreased baking sheets.

2. Brush cutouts lightly with oil; sprinkle with desired toppings.

3. Bake 6 to 8 minutes or until golden. Serve warm or at room temperature.

Tip: Puff pastry is prepared by layering thin sheets of pastry dough with bits of butter and then rolling and folding. The moisture in the melting butter creates steam which causes the pastry to puff and separate into crispy layers when it is baked.

Cheese Pinecones

Makes 12 to 16 servings

2 cups (8 ounces) shredded Swiss cheese
½ cup (1 stick) butter, softened
3 tablespoons milk
2 tablespoons dry sherry or milk
⅛ teaspoon ground red pepper
1 cup finely chopped blanched almonds
¾ cup slivered blanched almonds
¾ cup sliced almonds
½ cup whole almonds
Fresh rosemary sprigs (optional)
Assorted crackers

1. Beat cheese, butter, milk, sherry and red pepper in medium bowl with electric mixer at low speed until smooth; stir in chopped almonds.

2. Divide mixture into 3 equal portions; shape each into tapered oval to resemble pinecone. Insert slivered, sliced or whole almonds into each cone. Cover; refrigerate 2 to 3 hours or until firm.

3. Arrange cheese balls on wooden board or serving plate. Garnish with rosemary. Serve with assorted crackers.

Spicy, Sweet & Sour Cocktail Franks

Makes about 4 dozen cocktail franks

2 packages (8 ounces each) cocktail franks
½ cup ketchup or chili sauce
½ cup apricot preserves
1 teaspoon hot pepper sauce
Additional hot pepper sauce (optional)

SLOW COOKER DIRECTIONS

1. Combine all ingredients in 1½-quart slow cooker; mix well.

2. Cover; cook on LOW 2 to 3 hours.

3. Serve warm or at room temperature with additional hot pepper sauce, if desired.

Prep Time: 8 minutes
Cook Time: 2 to 3 hours

Yolkensteins

Makes 8 servings

8 hard-cooked eggs
8 small tomato slices
8 wooden toothpicks
    Mayonnaise
8 pimiento-stuffed olives
8 black peppercorns
    Parsley
16 whole cloves

1. Cut thin slice from wide end of egg so it stands upright. Slice egg horizontally, about ⅓ up from bottom.

2. Place tomato slice on bottom piece of egg. Insert toothpick upright in middle of tomato slice and egg for "spine." Reattach top piece of egg.

3. Use mayonnaise to attach slices of olives for eyes and peppercorn for nose. Attach parsley for hair and stick 1 whole clove on each side of egg under tomato slice for bolts. Place mayonnaise into pastry bag fitted with writing tip. Pipe mayonnaise teeth on tomato slice just before serving. Repeat for all eggs.

SERVING SUGGESTION:
Try serving these frightfully good treats to your kids for Halloween breakfast! Put out tiny plates of seasoned salt, sesame seeds, grated cheese and celery salt for dipping.

Abracadabra Hats

Makes 8 servings

1 package (8 ounces) crescent dinner roll dough
½ teaspoon dried basil
16 turkey pepperoni slices
3 to 4 salami sticks, cut into 2-inch pieces
2 cups pizza or marinara sauce

1. Preheat oven to 375°F. Separate dough and place individual pieces on work surface. Gently shape each piece into long triangle. Sprinkle triangles evenly with basil.

2. Cut pepperoni slices into crescent shapes using small cookie cutter or knife. (Each slice will make 2 crescents). Place 1 salami stick piece along base of each dough triangle. Partially roll up dough to cover salami and create brim of hat.

3. Place 2 pepperoni crescents on top part of each hat; place on ungreased nonstick baking sheet. Bake 12 minutes or until edges are golden brown. Meanwhile, warm sauce in small saucepan over low heat. Serve hats with warm pizza sauce for dipping.

Festive Franks

Makes 16 servings

1 package (8 ounces) refrigerated crescent roll dough

5½ teaspoons barbecue sauce

⅓ cup finely shredded sharp Cheddar cheese

8 hot dogs

¼ teaspoon poppy seeds (optional)

Additional barbecue sauce (optional)

1. Preheat oven to 350°F. Spray baking sheet with nonstick cooking spray; set aside.

2. Unroll dough and separate into 8 triangles. Cut each triangle in half lengthwise to make 2 triangles. Lightly spread barbecue sauce over each triangle. Sprinkle with cheese.

3. Cut each hot dog in half; trim off rounded ends. Place one hot dog piece at large end of one dough triangle. Roll up jelly-roll style from wide end. Place point-side down on prepared baking sheet. Sprinkle with poppy seeds. Repeat with remaining dough and hot dog pieces. Bake 13 minutes or until golden brown. Cool 1 to 2 minutes on baking sheet. Serve with additional barbecue sauce for dipping.

Eggy Eyeballs

Makes 24 servings

12 hard-cooked eggs,
   peeled and halved
   lengthwise
1 (8-ounce) package
   cream cheese
½ cup finely chopped
   yellow onion
½ cup finely chopped ham
   or turkey
¼ cup milk
⅛ teaspoon salt
⅛ teaspoon garlic powder
24 small pimiento-stuffed
   green olives
   Shredded red cabbage
12 carrots, halved

1. Remove egg yolks from egg halves; reserve yolks for another use. Combine cream cheese, onion, ham, milk, salt and garlic powder in small bowl; mix until well blended.

2. Fill each egg center with about 1 tablespoon of cream cheese mixture. Place olive (pimiento straight up) in center of each egg. Press slightly.

3. Place cabbage on serving platter, arrange egg halves on top in pairs. Place 1 carrot half below the center of each pair to resemble nose.

Celebration Cheese Ball

Makes about 2½ cups spread

2 packages (8 ounces each) cream cheese, softened
⅓ cup mayonnaise
¼ cup grated Parmesan cheese
2 tablespoons finely chopped carrot
1 tablespoon finely chopped red onion
1½ teaspoons prepared horseradish
¼ teaspoon salt
½ cup chopped pecans or walnuts
Assorted crackers and breadsticks

1. Combine all ingredients except pecans and crackers in medium bowl. Cover and refrigerate until firm.

2. Shape cheese mixture into ball; roll in pecans. Wrap cheese ball in plastic wrap and refrigerate at least 1 hour.

3. Serve with assorted crackers and breadsticks.

Acknowledgments

The publisher would like to thank the companies and organizations listed below for the use of their recipes and photographs in this publication.

Hillshire Farm®

Ortega®, A Division of B&G Foods, Inc.

Reckitt Benckiser Inc.

Unilever

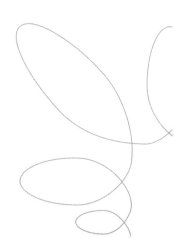

METRIC CONVERSION CHART

VOLUME MEASUREMENTS (dry)

1/8 teaspoon = 0.5 mL
1/4 teaspoon = 1 mL
1/2 teaspoon = 2 mL
3/4 teaspoon = 4 mL
1 teaspoon = 5 mL
1 tablespoon = 15 mL
2 tablespoons = 30 mL
1/4 cup = 60 mL
1/3 cup = 75 mL
1/2 cup = 125 mL
2/3 cup = 150 mL
3/4 cup = 175 mL
1 cup = 250 mL
2 cups = 1 pint = 500 mL
3 cups = 750 mL
4 cups = 1 quart = 1 L

VOLUME MEASUREMENTS (fluid)

1 fluid ounce (2 tablespoons) = 30 mL
4 fluid ounces (1/2 cup) = 125 mL
8 fluid ounces (1 cup) = 250 mL
12 fluid ounces (1 1/2 cups) = 375 mL
16 fluid ounces (2 cups) = 500 mL

WEIGHTS (mass)

1/2 ounce = 15 g
1 ounce = 30 g
3 ounces = 90 g
4 ounces = 120 g
8 ounces = 225 g
10 ounces = 285 g
12 ounces = 360 g
16 ounces = 1 pound = 450 g

DIMENSIONS

1/16 inch = 2 mm
1/8 inch = 3 mm
1/4 inch = 6 mm
1/2 inch = 1.5 cm
3/4 inch = 2 cm
1 inch = 2.5 cm

OVEN TEMPERATURE

250°F = 120°C
275°F = 140°C
300°F = 150°C
325°F = 160°C
350°F = 180°C
375°F = 190°C
400°F = 200°C
425°F = 220°C
450°F = 230°C

BAKING PAN SIZES

Utensil	Size in Inches/Quarts	Metric Volume	Size in Centimeters
Baking or	8×8×2	2 L	20×20×
Cake Pan	9×9×2	2.5 L	23×23×
(square or	12×8×2	3 L	30×20×
rectangular)	13×9×2	3.5 L	33×23×
Loaf Pan	8×4×3	1.5 L	20×10×
	9×5×3	2 L	23×13×
Round Layer	8×1½	1.2 L	20×4
Cake Pan	9×1½	1.5 L	23×4
Pie Plate	8×1¼	750 mL	20×3
	9×1¼	1 L	23×3
Baking Dish	1 quart	1 L	—
or Casserole	1½ quart	1.5 L	—
	2 quart	2 L	—